SCIENTIFIC AMERICAN

MORE
WINNING
SCIENCE
FAIR
PROJECTS

Grades
5-7

SCIENTIFIC AMERICAN

MORE WINNING SCIENCE FAIR PROJECTS

Grades 5-7

by Salvatore Tocci

Illustrated by Bob Wiacek

CHELSEA CLUBHOUSE

An Imprint of Chelsea House Publishers

For Rafe Statfeld Recanati

whose love of science was most evident as we worked through the investigations in this book. His inquisitive mind and interest in experimenting were invaluable in refining the investigative procedures so that they are clear to follow and easy to implement. Any student who approaches this book with the same attitude and curiosity as Rafe possesses is sure to find that his or her adventure will be an educational experience.

Scientific American: More Winning Science Fair Projects

Copyright © 2006 by Byron Preiss Visual Publications, Inc.
In cooperation with Scientific American and Chelsea House Publishers
Published in the United States of America in 2006 by Chelsea House Publishers.

Chelsea Clubhouse
An imprint of Chelsea House Publishers
132 West 31st Street
New York NY 10001

Library of Congress Cataloging-in-Publication Data
Tocci, Salvatore.
  Scientific American : more winning science fair projects, grades 5-7 / by Salvatore Tocci ; illustrated by Bob Wiacek.
    p. cm.
  ISBN 0-7910-9057-4
  1. Science projects—Juvenile literature. I. Title: More winning science fair projects, grades 5-7. II. Wiacek, Bob, ill. III. Scientific American, inc. IV. Title.
  Q182.3.T636 2006
  507'.8--dc22   2005057098

Chelsea House books are available at special discounts when purchased in bulk quantities for businesses, associations, institutions, or sales promotions. Please call our Special Sales Department in New York at (212) 967-8800 or (800) 322-8755.

You can find Chelsea House on the World Wide Web at
http://www.chelseahouse.com

Edited by Kate Nunn
Cover design by Andy Davies
Interior design by Gilda Hannah
Interior illustrations by Bob Wiacek

Printed in the United States of America

Bang PKG 10 9 8 7 6 5 4 3

This book is printed on acid-free paper.

CONTENTS

Science writer **Salvatore Tocci** was a high school biology and chemistry teacher for almost 30 years. Now an accomplished author of science-fact books for readers of all ages, his published work includes a high school chemistry textbook, a series of biographies of famous scientists, and two series for young readers on science experiments and chemical elements. He also travels throughout the country to present workshops at national science conventions.

RESOURCES FOR SCIENCE FAIR EXPERIMENTS

Supplies. All of the materials required for the experiments in this book can be found at home or in "houseware supplies" stores and "hardware" stores.

Information and further ideas. It is recommended that readers visit one or more of the following World Wide Web sites for more information on the science involved in this book's experiments, as well as for ideas for other experiments in the same areas of science. If you do not have a computer with an Internet hookup at home, try your school or local library.

http://www.ipl.org/div/kidspace/projectguide/
http://www.sciserv.org/isef/
http://energyquest.ca.gov/projects/index.html
http://www.ars.usda.gov/is/kids/fair/ideasframe.htm
http://kids.gov/k_science.htm
http://canadaonline.about.com/cs/sciencefairideas/
http://www.physics.uwo.ca/sfair/sflinks.htm
http://www.cdli.ca/sciencefairs/
http://www.scifair.org
http://homeworkspot.com/sciencefair/
http://school.discovery.com/sciencefaircentral/scifairstudio/ideas.html
http://www.all-science-fair-projects.com/category0.html

Have Fun with Your Science Fair Project

Y ou can learn science by reading about it in a book, magazine, or newspaper. However, the best way to learn science is by doing experiments. Not only is doing science experiments more fun, it is also the only way to learn how scientists work. You will find 36 science experiments in this book. Everything you need to do these experiments can be found in your home or at a local supermarket or hardware store.

Every experiment in this book must be done *with the help of an adult*. Both you and the adult should start by reading the *Background Information, Hypothesis, Materials*, and *Procedure* that appear at the start of each experiment. These sections will give you a clear idea of what the experiment is about, the materials you will need to do it, and the steps you must follow. In some experiments, the *Procedure* will point out that you need the adult to perform a certain step. For example, the *Procedure* may require the use of a sharp knife or hot stove. The adult should perform these

steps. However, remember that you must have an adult supervise *all* your work in *every* experiment.

Another safety step is to wear something to protect your eyes while you are doing an experiment. Some of the chemicals used in certain experiments can irritate your eyes if they accidentally splash on your face. If you don't have them handy, you can buy safety goggles in a hardware store.

Before you do any of the experiments in this book, you should get a notebook to write down the results you get and observations you make. This should be your "lab notebook," where you only keep information that deals with your experiments. Try to keep it as organized as possible so that you can easily locate the information if you need it later.

Think of each experiment as the starting point for learning something about science. For example, you may do the experiment under the heading *Energy*. This experiment shows you how to

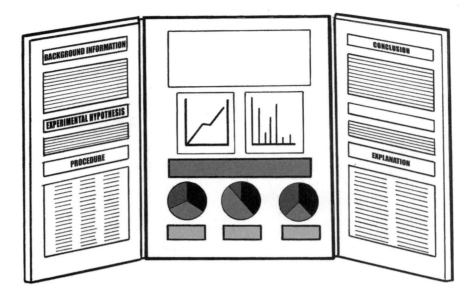

release the energy stored in a peanut. After you finish this experiment, you can try releasing the energy in other types of nuts or other foods that are fairly easy to burn, such as potato chips. Like any good scientist, you should also be creative. For example, can you design and build your own device that can measure how much energy is released when a peanut burns?

If you design your own experiment, be sure that you do so correctly. When a scientist designs an experiment, he or she always includes a control. A control in an experiment is set up so that only one variable is introduced by the scientist. A variable is anything that changes. For example, consider the experiment titled *Preservatives*. This experiment involves setting up three jars. Each jar contains the same amount of chicken bouillon. All three jars are left standing for the same length of time and at the same temperature. However, salt is added to one jar, vinegar to a second jar, while nothing is added to the third jar. The third jar serves as the control. All three jars are identical except for one thing. This is the variable. In one jar, the variable is salt. In another jar, the variable is vinegar.

If the jar with the salt added looks different from the control jar, then the salt must have been the cause of the change. The same is true of the jar with the vinegar added. The temperature and the time could not have been responsible because all three jars were exposed to the same temperature and for the same length of time. Having the proper control allows the experimenter to identify what was responsible for any change that might be observed.

If you wish, you can use an experiment as a project for your school's science fair. The more information you present in your project, the more interesting it will be. Use an experiment in this book as your starting point. You can then expand the experiment by testing other items. For example, you may do the secondary experiment with vinegar and pennies in *Physical and Chemical Changes*. You can expand this experiment by testing what happens when you use other household solutions such as lemon juice and seltzer water in place of vinegar.

Tips for Your Tabletop Display

Students usually present their science fair projects in the form of a three-sided display. All the important information from the project is shown on this display. The left hand side of the display can include some background information about your experiment. Place the hypothesis that you investigated underneath this information. Then include the procedure you followed.

Place the title, your name, and grade at the

top of the center of the display. Include all the results you collected. You may simply display the results as you wrote them down in your notebook. However, try to make the display more appealing by including colorful charts and tables of your results.

Showing Your Data

You can include any photographs or drawings that illustrate your procedure on the center

DISTANCE CUP MOVES

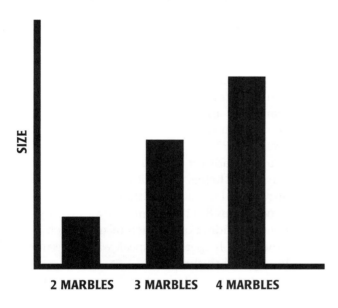

RADIOACTIVITY

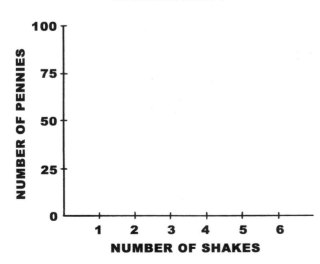

panel. You may want to use a graph to display your data. There are many types of graphs, but two that you may find useful are bar graphs and line graphs.

When you perform the experiment with marbles in *Momentum*, you can make a bar chart showing how far the cup moves when you release two, three, and four marbles down the ramp.

If you perform the experiment with pennies in *Radioactivity*, you can make a line graph by plotting the number of tosses along the X-axis and the number of pennies along the Y-axis.

Explaining Your Results

The right hand side of the display usually includes the results of your experiment as you wrote them down in your notebook. Place your conclusion and explanation underneath the results. Your display will be more impressive if you include information that you discovered on your own. For example, search the Internet for additional information to include in the background information or explanation. Your display will also be more impressive if you show the setup that you used in your experiment. The equipment is usually displayed on the tabletop in front of the three-sided display.

You can also check your school library and the Internet for additional information on how to present your project at a science fair.

Show Time!

When it is time for you to present your display to an audience, you need to walk them carefully through your experiment. Move from your left panel, to the center, and then to the right panel. Start by telling your audience the question you asked and taking them through your procedure. Then talk about your data. Explain it fully to them by adding details of your recordings in your lab book. Finally, what conclusion did you come to after doing your experiment? No matter how you present your project, make sure to impress your audience with what you learned and how much fun you had while learning it!

Why Do You Need Two Ears?

BACKGROUND INFORMATION

Have you ever heard the expression "Two heads are better than one?" Do you think it might it also be true that two ears are better than one? Obviously, our ears detect sounds. A sound consists of waves that travel through a medium, such as air or water. When these waves reach the ear, they cause the eardrum to vibrate. In turn, these vibrations cause tiny bones in a structure called the middle ear to vibrate. These vibrations send messages to the brain.

The brain interprets these messages as the sounds we hear. The messages may be interpreted as the sound of a bird singing in a tree or the sound of a car driving down the road. Our ears can detect thousands of different sounds. But why do we have *two* ears? For one thing, two ears allow us to hear stereophonic sounds. In other words, one ear picks up one sound, while another ear picks up a different sound. You sense this whenever you put on two earphones to listen to music. The following experiment will show you that there is another advantage to having two ears. You should do this experiment when there is as little noise as possible around you.

Hypothesis

Two ears are better than one to judge distance.

Materials

- Helper
- Tape or chalk
- Large open space such as a school gymnasium or a parking lot
- Measuring tape
- Cotton
- Pencil
- Paper

Procedure

1. Use tape or chalk to mark an X on the floor or ground.
2. Measure 5 feet from this spot and mark another X at this point.
3. Continue in a straight line to measure and mark a spot every 5 feet. You should mark six spots. The sixth and last spot will be 30 feet from the original X.
4. Stand on the original X and face the other marks placed on the ground.
5. Carefully place a piece of cotton in your left ear.
6. Cover your left ear with your hand and tightly close your eyes.
7. Your helper should move to one of the spots marked by an X.
8. Your helper should face you and ask "How far away am I?"
9. You must answer 5, 10, 15, 20, 25, or 30 feet.
10. Have your helper write down both your answer and the actual distance.
11. Repeat steps 8–11 three more times with your helper standing on a different mark each time. Your helper must speak with the same loudness each time.
12. Repeat steps 5–12, this time covering your right ear.
13. Repeat steps 5–12, this time using both ears.
14. Compare your results for the three trials.

Results

One ear is probably no better than the other in judging how far away a sound is coming from. However, most people guess closer to the actual distance when both ears are used.

Conclusion and Explanation

The closer a sound is, the louder it sounds. Two ears are better than one in distinguishing between sounds with different loudness. Therefore, using two ears enables us to judge distance better than with one ear.

Both bats and dolphins depend on sounds to determine distances. These animals emit sounds through their mouths. These sounds bounce off an object and then echo back to the animal's sensitive ears. The animal's brain then translates the time it takes to hear the echo into how far away the object is.

SECONDARY EXPERIMENT

Have you ever heard a noise and could not tell where it was coming from? For example, you may forget where you've put your cell phone. When it rings, you might have to go searching to locate it. The loudness of the ringing gives you a clue as to how far away the cell phone is. But having two ears also makes it easier to tell where the ringing is coming from.

Materials
- Helper
- Tape or chalk
- Large, open space such as a school gymnasium or a parking lot
- Measuring tape
- Cotton
- Pencil
- Paper

Procedure

Use tape or chalk to mark an X on the floor or ground.

1. Measure 20 feet from this spot and mark another X at this point.
2. Repeat step 2 to make a series of Xs that form a circle around the original X. Each X must be 20 feet from the central X but located in a different direction.
3. Stand on the X in the center.
4. Carefully place a piece of cotton in your left ear.
5. Cover your left ear with your hand and tightly close your eyes.
6. Your helper should move to one of the other Xs.
7. Your helper should face you and ask, "Where am I?"
8. You must point to the person.
9. Have your helper draw their location on a piece of paper and the direction you pointed to.
10. Repeat steps 7–10 five more times with your helper standing on a different mark each time. Your helper must speak with the same loudness each time.
11. Repeat steps 4–11, this time covering your right ear.
12. Repeat steps 4–11, this time using both ears.

Results

One ear is probably no better than the other in judging where a sound is coming from. However, most people guess closer to the actual location when both ears are used.

Conclusion and Explanation

With two ears open, a sound may not reach each ear at the same time. For example, a sound coming directly from your left reaches your left ear about 500 microseconds before it reaches your right ear. A microsecond is one-millionth of a second. As a result, your left ear sends a signal to your brain a fraction of a second sooner than your right ear. Your brain uses this difference in time to determine the location of the sound. If only one ear is used, the brain doesn't receive two signals at different times. As a result, the brain cannot determine the location of the sound.

What Is Potential Energy?

BACKGROUND INFORMATION

Scientists define energy as the ability to do some type of work. You know that you need energy to move a muscle. However, did you know that you need energy to see with your eyes, think with your brain, and pump blood through your body? In fact, everything you do, even if you are not aware of it, requires energy. This energy comes from the foods you eat.

The energy in foods comes from the chemical substances they contain. Foods contain three major types of chemical substances, which include proteins, carbohydrates, and lipids (fats). The energy contained, or stored, in these chemical substances is called potential energy. The word potential means "the ability to do something." Therefore, potential energy has the ability to do some type of work. This work includes everything you do, such as move, see, and think. All that has to be done is to release the potential energy stored in the foods. The following experiment shows how you can release this potential energy to do some work. In this case, the work involves raising the temperature of water.

Hypothesis

The potential energy stored in a food can be released to do some type of work.

Materials

- Adult helper
- Sewing needle
- Cork
- Unsalted, shelled peanuts
- Hammer
- Large nail
- Two empty juice or soda cans; one must be small enough to fit inside the other
- Can opener
- Metal skewer
- Hot plate
- Measuring cup marked in milliliters (mL)
- Thermometer marked in Celsius (°C)
- Lighter

Procedure

1. Insert the eye of the needle into the cork.
2. Carefully insert the pointed end of the needle into the peanut. Insert the needle so that the

peanut points slightly upward. If the peanut breaks, try another one until you have a whole peanut inserted into the needle.

3. Use the hammer and nail to punch holes around the outside of the larger can near the bottom.
4. Use the can opener to remove both the top and bottom of the larger can.
5. Use the can opener to remove only the top from the smaller can.
6. Use the hammer and nail to punch two holes in the smaller can. These holes should be near the top and exactly opposite others.
7. Insert the metal skewer through the two holes in the smaller can.
8. Rest the smaller can on the top of the larger can.
9. Place the cork and peanut on the hot plate. The bottom of the smaller can must rest just above the peanut. You may have to make two new holes in the smaller can.
10. Pour 50 mL of water into the smaller can.
11. Insert the thermometer into the water. Record the water temperature.
12. Remove the cans from the hot plate.
13. Ask the adult to use the lighter so that the peanut starts burning. Keep trying because the peanut will not burn easily.
14. As soon as the peanut is burning, put both cans back on the hot plate.
15. Allow the peanut to burn completely.
16. Use the thermometer to stir the water gently.
17. Record the water temperature.

Results

The water temperature increases as the peanut burns. You can calculate how much potential energy is released by the burning peanut. Energy can be measured in calories. A calorie is defined as the amount of energy that is required to raise the temperature of 1 gram (g) of water by 1°C. At room temperature, 1 g of water is almost equal to 1 mL of water. Therefore, you can assume that you have 50 g (50 mL) of water.

Also assume that the temperature rises from 18°C to 38°C, which is an increase of 20°C. In this example, the number of calories is calculated as follows: 50 g x 20°C = 1000 calories. Calculate how many calories were produced in your experiment.

Conclusion and Explanation

As the peanut burns, the potential energy stored in the peanut is released. The potential energy that is released changes into heat energy. This heat energy raises the water temperature. How much the temperature increases depends on several factors: how completely the peanut burns and how close the burning peanut is to the water in the smaller can.

SECONDARY EXPERIMENT

Potential energy can be found everywhere you look. A leaf on a tree, a glass on a table, and a ball at the top of the stairs all have potential energy. The leaf may fall, the glass may drop to the floor, and the ball may roll down the stairs. When they do, their potential energy is changed into another form of energy, called kinetic energy. Kinetic energy is commonly called energy of motion.

Changing potential energy into kinetic energy can be fun. For example, a roller coaster changes potential energy into kinetic energy. At the top of the ride, the roller coaster has potential energy. The rest of the ride depends on changing this potential energy into kinetic energy. The following experiment will explore what happens as potential energy is changed into kinetic energy on a roller coaster.

Materials
• Tape
• Long piece of clear flexible plastic tubing
• Flat wall surface
• Marble that can roll freely inside the plastic tubing

Procedure
1. Tape the plastic tubing to the wall to form a U-shape.

2. Insert the marble into the plastic tubing. Use a piece of tape to mark how high the marble rolls up the other side of the tubing.
3. Repeat step 2 several times.
4. Tape the plastic tubing so that it forms a small hill near the bottom.
5. Repeat steps 2–3.
6. Tape the plastic tubing so that it forms a loop that is higher than where the marble stops.
7. Repeat steps 2–3.
8. Tape the plastic tubing so that it forms a loop whose height is lower than where the marble stops.
9. Watch what happens to the marble.

Results

The marble stops at the same height even if there is a small hill or loop along its path. However, if the loop is lower than the height the marble normally reaches, then the marble makes it com-pletely around the loop and falls out of the plastic tubing.

Conclusion and Explanation

At the top of the plastic tubing, the marble has potential energy. When you release the marble, this potential energy is changed into kinetic energy. This kinetic energy propels the marble over a hill and up a loop. In every case, the marble reaches the same height. However, the marble never reaches the same height as where it started.

If potential energy is changed into kinetic energy, then why doesn't the marble reach the same height as where it started? As the marble travels through the plastic tubing, there is something else involved: friction. Friction is a force that slows down and eventually stops a moving object. Imagine how much more fun a roller coaster would be if there were no friction to slow down the cars. The hills and loops could be made even higher.

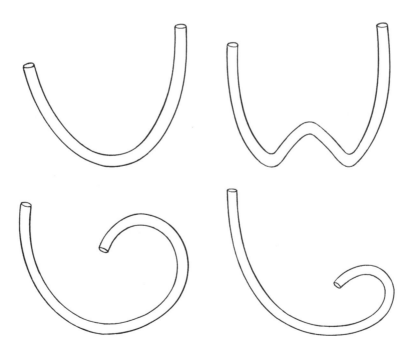

How Can You Use a Battery to Make a Magnet?

BACKGROUND INFORMATION

Look around your house and you'll notice how useful electricity is for doing many things. Without electricity, the lights, radios, televisions, computers, appliances, and clocks would not be working. Look around your house again and count how many magnets are being used. You may see magnets holding pictures and drawings on the refrigerator door. However, you probably will not notice any other ways in which magnets are used.

Yet, magnets are just as useful as electricity. Magnets are used in speakers, doorbells, televisions, and kitchen appliances. These magnets are different from the ones on a refrigerator door. Magnets that hold objects against a refrigerator door are called permanent magnets. Magnets that are used elsewhere in the house are called electromagnets. Both types of magnets create a force known as a magnetic field.

As its name suggests, an electromagnet involves both electricity and magnetism. Electricity is used to turn a metal object, such as a coil of wire, into a magnet. Electromagnets are useful when you don't need a magnet all the time. As long as electricity is flowing, the coil acts like a magnet. When the electricity is shut off, the coil no longer operates like a magnet.

Procedure

1. Place the magnet near the aluminum foil to see if the two attract each other.
2. Stand the two books upright on a flat surface, about 12 inches apart.
3. Tape the ends of the ruler to the top of each book.
4. Cut a strip of aluminum foil about 2 feet long and 1 inch wide.
5. Tape one end of the foil strip to the underside of the ruler.
6. Tape the other end of the foil strip to the ruler, about 1 inch from the spot where the other end is taped. The foil should form a narrow loop hanging down from the ruler. Have the descending part of the loop be close to, but not touching, the ascending part of the loop.
7. Attach one alligator clip to each battery terminal.
8. Attach one alligator clip to one end of the foil taped to the ruler. Briefly touch the other alligator clip to the other end of the aluminum foil.
9. Watch what happens to the aluminum foil.
10. Disconnect the alligator clip from the foil.
11. Remove the tape from both ends of the foil.

Hypothesis

Electricity can be used to turn a non-magnetic metal into a magnet.

Materials

- Magnet
- Aluminum foil
- Two tall books of the same height
- Ruler
- Tape
- Scissors
- Two alligator clips
- 6-volt lantern battery

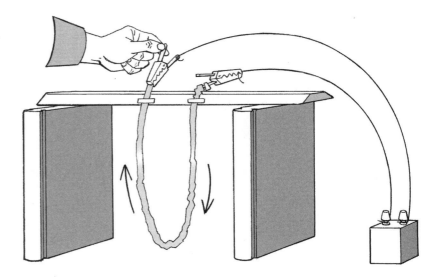

12. Tape both ends of the foil to the ruler so that they overlap.
13. Separate the two sides of the foil to make a loop.
14. Attach one alligator clip from the battery to the overlapping ends of the foil.
15. Briefly touch the other alligator clip from the battery to the bottom of the loop.
16. Watch what happens to the aluminum foil.

Results
The magnet does not attract the aluminum foil. When the foil ends do not overlap, the descending and ascending parts of the loop repel each other. As a result, the two parts of the loop move apart from each other. When the foil ends do overlap, the descending and ascending parts of the loop attract each other. As a result, the two parts of the loop move toward each other.

Conclusion and Explanation
Aluminum is not magnetic. Electricity supplied by the battery turns the aluminum foil into a magnet. When the foil ends do not overlap, electricity from the battery travels down one part of the aluminum loop and up the other part of the aluminum loop. If electricity flows in opposite directions through the aluminum foil loop, then

the two parts repel each other. This is what happens when you bring the north poles or the south poles of two magnets together.

When the ends of the aluminum foil overlap, electricity from the battery flows through the ascending and descending loop in the same direction. If electricity flows in the same direction through the aluminum foil loop, then the two parts attract each other. This is what happens when you bring the north pole of one magnet close to the south pole of another magnet. Therefore, the two loops of aluminum acts like a pair of magnets.

SECONDARY EXPERIMENT

A compass points north because Earth acts like a giant magnet. However, you can make a magnet that is even more powerful than Earth.

Materials
- Two tall books of the same height
- Piece of poster board, 12 inches by 12 inches
- Wire cutters
- Uncoated wire hanger
- Metal file
- Compass

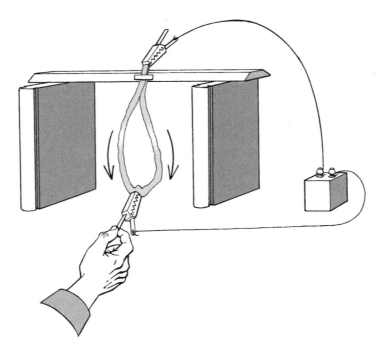

Procedure

1. Stand the two books upright on a flat surface, about 12 inches apart.
2. Tape the ends of the poster board to the top of each book.
3. Cut a straight piece of metal from the wire hanger.
4. Insert the metal wire through the center of the poster board so that it stands upright.
5. Place the compass near the metal piece. Observe the direction in which the needle points.
6. Attach one alligator clip to each battery terminal.
7. Attach one alligator clip to the bottom end of the metal wire.
8. Briefly touch the other alligator clip to the top end of the metal wire.
9. Observe the direction in which the compass needle points.
10. Repeat steps 6–10, moving the compass around the metal wire.

Results

The compass needle points north. However, when the wire is connected to the battery, the compass needle points in different directions as you move it around the wire.

Conclusions

Electricity from the battery turns the metal wire into an electromagnet. This electromagnet creates a magnetic field that is stronger than Earth's. Therefore, the compass needle responds to the magnetic field created by the wire and not to Earth's magnetic field. Although it may be stronger, the magnetic force from the electromagnet extends for only a short distance beyond the wire. In contrast, Earth's magnetic force extends all over the world.

Which Way Does Water Move?

BACKGROUND INFORMATION

All plants and animals are made up of one or more small units called cells. Cells must get the water and nutrients they need to survive and grow. Cells must also get rid of toxic wastes. Water, nutrients, and wastes are constantly moving into and out of cells. These substances move in several ways. Two ways include diffusion and osmosis.

Diffusion is the movement of a substance from an area of higher concentration to an area of lower concentration. Diffusion can easily be demonstrated by opening a bottle of ammonia. The ammonia diffuses from the container, where it is highly concentrated. As a result, the first person to smell the ammonia is the one who opens the container. The next person to smell the ammonia is someone standing nearby. A person standing farthest from the open container would be the last one to smell it because it takes longer for the ammonia to diffuse to where the person is standing.

Osmosis is the diffusion of water across a barrier, such as a membrane that surrounds a cell. Water always moves by osmosis from an area of higher concentration to an area of lower concentration. If allowed to continue, both diffusion and osmosis will result in equal concentrations throughout an area or on either side of a cell membrane.

Hypothesis

Water will move by osmosis from an area of higher concentration to an area of lower concentration.

Materials

- Kitchen scale
- Gummy bears
- Drinking glass
- Paper towel

Procedure

1. Place enough bears on the scale so that you get a reading. Write down how much they weigh.
2. Place the bears in the glass and cover with water.
3. Allow them to soak for 24 hours.
4. Pour off the water and place the bears on the paper towel.
5. Describe any changes in their appearance.
6. Again weigh the bears.

Results

The bears are larger and weigh more after being in the water for 24 hours.

Conclusion and Explanation

Water is in a higher concentration outside the gummer bears. As a result, water moves by osmosis into the bears. Because they gain water, the bears get larger and weigh more.

SECONDARY EXPERIMENT

Concentration is not the only factor that affects diffusion and osmosis. Another factor is surface area. As its name suggests, surface area is the amount of exposed area that an object has. Consider two cubes. One cube measures 1 inch on each side. The other cube measures 2 inches on each side.

The surface area of one side of the 1-inch cube equals 1 in x 1 in or 1 in^2. Because there are six sides, the total surface area equals 6 x 1 in^2 or 6 in^2. The volume of the 1-inch cube equals 1 in x 1 in x 1 in or 1 in^3. For the 1-inch cube, the surface area to volume ratio is 6:1 (6 in^2: 1 in^3).

The surface area of one side of the 2-inch cube equals 2 in x 2 in or 4 in^2. Because there are six sides, the total surface area equals 6 x 4 in^2 or 24 in^2. The volume of the 2-inch cube equals 2 in x 2 in x 2 in or 8 in^3. For the 2-inch cube, the surface area to volume ratio is 3:1 (24 in^2: 8 in^3).

Therefore, the smaller cube has a higher ratio of surface area to volume than the larger cube. The following experiment shows how this ratio affects diffusion and osmosis.

Materials
- Adult helper
- Knife
- Red cabbage
- Measuring cup
- Large pot
- Stove
- Cheesecloth or coffee filter
- Rubber band
- Container
- Unflavored gelatin
- Deep tray or baking pan
- Ruler
- Refrigerator
- Drinking glass
- Tablespoon
- Liquid ammonia
- Paper towel

Procedure
1. Ask the adult to chop the cabbage into small pieces.
2. Add 2 cups of the cabbage to a large pot.
3. Cover the cabbage with water and boil for 10 minutes.
4. Allow the liquid to cool to room temperature.
5. Cover the container with a piece of cheesecloth or coffee filter. Use a rubber band to secure the cheesecloth or filter to the container.
6. Slowly pour the contents of the pot through a piece of cheesecloth or coffee filter.
7. Collect the purplish liquid in the container.
8. Prepare the gelatin according to the directions on the package. Add some of the purplish liquid from the red cabbage to the gelatin.
9. Pour the colored gelatin into the tray. The gelatin in the tray must be at least 1 inch thick.
10. Place the gelatin in a refrigerator until it solidifies.
11. Cut two gelatin cubes. One should measure ½ inch on each side. The other cube should measure 1 inch on each side.

12. Carefully place both gelatin cubes in the glass.
13. Cover the cubes with water and add 1 tablespoon of ammonia. Allow the cubes to soak for 10 minutes.
14. Carefully pour the liquid down a sink. Carefully rinse the cubes with water.
15. Place both cubes on a paper towel.
16. Cut both cubes in half.
17. Describe the appearance of each cube.

Results
Ammonia causes the pigment in red cabbage to turn green or yellowish-green.

The surfaces and interiors of both cubes appear greenish or yellowish-green. However, the color extends deeper into the ½-inch cube than it does into the 1-inch cube.

Conclusion and Explanation
Ammonia diffuses into both cubes, causing the red cabbage pigment to turn greenish. In the same amount of time, however, the ammonia diffuses farther into the smaller cube. The ammonia diffuses farther because the smaller cube has a higher ratio of surface area to volume than the larger cube.

Why Do Some Things Float in Water?

BACKGROUND INFORMATION

You know that if you toss a rock into water, it will sink. However, if you toss a cork, it will float. The reason a rock sinks while a cork floats has to do with their densities. Density is defined as the mass of an object divided by its volume. Mass is the amount of matter, or stuff, that an object has. Volume is the space that the object occupies.

Scientists express the values of densities in metric units: g (grams), mL (milliliters), and cc^3 (cubic centimeters). For example, the density of water is 1 g/mL or 1 g/cc^3. The word *per* is written as "/".

A rock sinks because its density is greater than 1 g/mL. In contrast, a cork floats because its density is less than 1 g/mL. The following experiment explores the densities of various liquids and solids.

3. Add five drops of red food coloring to the water and stir.
4. Tilt the glass and slowly pour the corn syrup down the inside of the glass.
5. Repeat step 4, first pouring the glycerin, then the water, and finally the vegetable oil. Pour each liquid slowly and carefully so that each one forms a separate layer.
6. Place each object, one at a time, on the surface of the vegetable oil.
7. Describe what happens to each object.

Results

From top to bottom, the four layers are oil, water, glycerin, and corn syrup. The results will vary when an object is placed on top of the oil.

Hypothesis

Density determines whether an object will sink or float in a liquid.

Materials

- Measuring cup
- Corn syrup
- Glycerin
- Vegetable oil
- Green and red food coloring
- Teaspoon
- Tall clear drinking glass
- Small household objects that can fit inside the drinking glass, such as a marble, penny, bottle cap, metal screw, and paper clip.

Procedure

1 Pour ¼ cup corn syrup, ¼ cup glycerin, ¼ cup water, and ¼ vegetable oil into four separate cups.
2. Add five drops of green food coloring to the corn syrup and stir. Rinse the spoon when you have finished stirring.

Conclusion and Explanation

Each of the four liquids has a different density. Because it has a lower density, the glycerin floats on the corn syrup. Because it has a lower density, the water floats on the corn syrup. Because it has the lowest density, the oil floats at the top. If its density is greater than the liquid, an object will sink. The greater its density, the deeper the object will sink in the glass. However, if its density is less than the liquid, the object will float. For example, if an object sinks in the water but floats in the glycerin, the density of the object is between 1.00 g/mL (the density of water) and 1.26 g/mL (the density of glycerin). If an object sinks to the bottom of the glass, its density is greater than 1.37 g/mL, which is the density of the corn syrup.

SECONDARY EXPERIMENT

You may think that any heavy, solid object will sink in water. However, ships float despite their heavy masses. They float because their densities are less than the density of water. Remember that a ship has a hull that is filled with air, which is much less dense than water. The combined density of the ship and air inside is less than the density of water.

But what about a heavy object that is not filled with air, such as a bowling ball? Can a bowling ball possibly float in water? If you know the density of the bowling ball, then you can predict whether it will float or sink. You can then perform the experiment to test your hypothesis.

Materials
- Bathroom scale
- Bowling ball that weighs 10 pounds or less (around 8 pounds works best)
- String
- Scissors
- Yardstick
- Calculator
- Bathtub

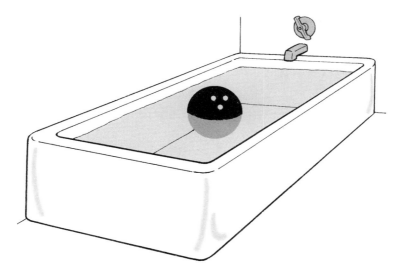

Procedure

1. Weigh yourself on the scale.
2. While holding the bowling ball, again weigh yourself on the scale.
3. Subtract the weight in step 1 from the weight in step 2. This value is the weight of the bowling ball. If the value is in pounds, multiply by 453.6 grams to convert to the metric value for mass. Record the mass of the bowling ball in grams.
4. Wrap a piece of string around the widest part of the bowling ball. This is its circumference. Cut the string and then lay it straight next to the yardstick. According to the rules, a bowling ball must have a circumference no greater than 27.002 inches or less than 26.704 inches. Therefore, the circumference should be close to 27 inches.
5. To convert to the metric system, 1 inch = 2.54 cm. Therefore, multiply the value in step 4 by 2.54 to convert it to centimeters. This value represents the circumference of the bowling bowl in centimeters.
6. The formula for circumference is: circumference = 2 times π times radius. The symbol π represents pi, which equals 3.14. Calculate the radius of the bowling ball as follows.

$$\text{radius} = \frac{\text{circumference [from step 5]}}{2\pi \text{ [which equals 6.28]}}$$

7. Next calculate the volume of the bowling ball by using the following formula. Notice that the value for the radius you calculated in step 6 is cubed in the following formula.

$$\text{volume} = 4/3 \times \pi \times \text{radius}^3$$

8. Divide the mass of the bowling ball (step 3) by the volume of the bowling ball (step 7). This value represents the density of the bowling ball in g/cc^3.
9. Predict whether the bowling ball will float or sink if you place it in water.

Results

The bowling ball should float in water.

Conclusion and Explanation

Because its density is less than 1.00 g/cc^3, the bowling ball floats in water. You can confirm this prediction by filling a bathtub with water and then gently lowering the bowling ball into the tub. Note that this experiment did not take into consideration the finger holes in the bowling ball. The volume of these finger holes should be subtracted from the volume you calculated for the bowling ball to get its actual volume. However, the volume of the finger holes is small enough to ignore. You can perform the same calculations to predict of a bowling ball heavier than 13 pounds will sink or float in water.

HOW CAN A PENNY SIGNAL A CHANGE?

BACKGROUND INFORMATION

Changes are constantly occurring around you. Many changes are noticeable. For example, you have seen ice melt and change into water. Other changes go unnoticed. For example, water is needed to change the foods you eat into the substances your body can use. These changes occur during digestion.

Ice melting is an example of a physical change. A physical change occurs without any change in the nature of the substance. Water is still water, no matter whether it is a solid or a liquid. In contrast, digestion is an example of a chemical change. A chemical change occurs when the nature of a substance changes. For example, digestion changes proteins into new substances called amino acids. The following experiment shows how to use a penny to tell that a physical change has occurred.

Hypothesis

Air can undergo a physical change.

Materials

- Empty glass soda bottle
- Large bucket or container
- Ice
- Penny

Procedure

1. Submerge the soda bottle in a bucket of ice for 2 minutes.
2. Remove the bottle from the ice.
3. Wet the mouth of the bottle with water.
4. Place the penny so that it completely covers the mouth of the bottle.
5. Wrap both your hands around the bottle.
6. Watch what happens to the penny.

Results

The penny jumps from the mouth of the bottle.

Conclusion and Explanation

The ice causes the air inside the bottle to get cold. Your hands cause the air to get warmer. Air is made of tiny particles called molecules. As the molecules in air get warmer, they move apart from one another or expand. As the warm air expands, it pushes up against the penny. As a result, the penny is pushed off the top of the bottle.

SECONDARY EXPERIMENT

A new penny is bright and shiny. In time, this penny will get dull and may even turn greenish. Pennies get dull over time because of a chemical change. Copper is a bright, shiny reddish metal that is used to make pennies. Copper slowly reacts with the oxygen in air to form a new substance. This new substance is called copper oxide. Copper oxide is a dull, greenish substance. See how you can get rid of the copper oxide so that you have a bright, shiny penny again.

Materials
- Teaspoon
- Salt
- Measuring cup
- White vinegar
- Glass or plastic bowl
- Tongs
- 21 dull pennies
- Clock or watch with second hand
- Paper towels
- Waterproof marker

Procedure
1. Dissolve 1 teaspoon of salt in ¼ cup of white vinegar.
2. Pour the liquid into the bowl.
3. Use the tongs to dip a penny halfway into the liquid and hold it there for 30 seconds.
4. Remove the penny and describe what you see.
5. Carefully dump the remaining pennies into the bowl. Allow the pennies to soak for 5 minutes.
6. While you are waiting, label one paper towel "not rinsed" and another paper towel "rinsed."
7. Use the tongs to remove 10 pennies and place them on a paper towel labeled "not rinsed."
8. Pour the liquid down the drain.
9. Thoroughly rinse the remaining 10 pennies in the bowl with tap water.
10. Place these pennies on the other paper towel.
11. Wait at least one hour and then describe the appearance of the pennies.

Results
The half of the penny that is dipped into the salt and vinegar appears bright and shiny. The pennies soaked in salt and vinegar and then rinsed with water remain bright. The pennies soaked in salt and vinegar but that are not rinsed start to turn dull.

Conclusion and Explanation
Pennies turn dull as a result of a chemical reaction. This chemical reaction changes the copper in a penny into copper oxide, a greenish substance. Vinegar contains a chemical substance called acetic acid. This acid dissolves copper oxide, exposing the bright, shiny copper beneath the copper oxide.

The pennies that are soaked in salt and vinegar and then rinsed with water are shiny at first but will in time turn dull again. This is a chemical change that takes place very slowly. The pennies that are soaked in salt and vinegar but not rinsed with water are also shiny at first. However, these pennies turn dull and greenish much quicker than the pennies that are not rinsed with water. The pennies that have not been rinsed with water are still coated with salt and vinegar. The vinegar and salt speed up the chemical change that turns shiny copper into dull copper oxide.

What Can a Penny Tell You About Radioactivity?

BACKGROUND INFORMATION

All matter is made from elements. An element is a substance that cannot be separated or be broken down into simpler substances by ordinary means. There are slightly more than 100 known elements. Each element exists in more than one form. The different forms of an element are called isotopes. Some isotopes are stable. In other words, they do not change no matter how much time passes. An isotope of carbon, known as carbon-12, is an example of a stable isotope. Other isotopes are unstable. These isotopes break down or decay. When they do, they give off radiation. An isotope of carbon, known as carbon-14, is an example of a radioactive isotope.

All radioactive isotopes have one common characteristic. They decay in a predictable manner. Each isotope has a certain half-life. A half-life is the amount of time it takes for one-half of a radioactive isotope to decay. For example, the half-life of carbon-14 is 5715 years. Assume that you have 10 pounds of carbon-14. In 5715 years, there will be 5 pounds remaining. After another 5715 years, there will be only 2.5 pounds left, and so on.

Scientists sometimes make models to help them in their work. Such models can be quite sophisticated and complicated. These models are usually created with a computer. In contrast, some models can be very simple. For example, a penny can be used as a model of a radioactive isotope that decays.

Hypothesis

Pennies can serve as models to demonstrate the concept of a half-life.

Materials

- 200 pennies
- Plastic container with lid
- Clock or watch with second hand
- Unlined paper
- Ruler
- Pencil

Procedure

1. Place the pennies in the container and cover.
2. Shake the pennies by repeatedly turning the container upside down and back up for 5 seconds.
3. Open the container and spill the pennies on a flat surface.
4. Remove all the pennies that are heads up.
5. Count the number of pennies that are left and place them back in the container.
6. Repeat steps 2–5 until there are no pennies left to place back in the container.
7. Make a graph of your results. Plot the number of shakes along the horizontal axis and the pennies left along the vertical axis.
8. Repeat steps 1–7, but this time, shake the pennies for 10 seconds.

Results

Approximately half the pennies are removed after each shake of the container. Eventually, no pennies remain.

Conclusion and Explanation

Pennies can be used to model what happens to a radioactive isotope. In the real world, a radioactive isotope decays so that only half the original amount remains after a certain time. In the experiment, the pennies represent atoms of a radioactive isotope. Each toss represents the half-life. The pennies that land heads up represent atoms that have decayed. Approximately half the pennies (atoms) decay after each toss (half-life).

Different radioactive isotopes have different half-lives. In the first trial, the half-life was 5 seconds. In the second trial, the pennies were used to model a different radioactive isotope. This radioactive isotope has a half life of 10 seconds. Yet, both isotopes decayed so that only half the original amount remained after each had gone through one half-life.

SECONDARY EXPERIMENT

Radioactive isotopes are found everywhere on Earth, including the land, sea, and air. As a result, all living things are exposed to these radioactive isotopes. Fortunately, the level of exposure to this natural radiation does not pose a health risk. However, some people are exposed to elevated levels of radiation that can be hazardous. These people include those who work in hospitals and research labs where radioactive isotopes are regularly used for testing and treatment. These people take precautions so that they are not exposed to the radiation. In addition, they wear special badges that monitor their exposure.

Homes can also be places where elevated levels of radiation exist. This radiation comes from a gas called radon. Radon has been found in homes all over the country. Uranium that is in soil, rock, and water decays. As the uranium decays, radon forms. This radon seeps through cracks and other tiny openings in the foundation. Because radon gas is heavy, it collects in basements where its level slowly increases. Radon is colorless, odorless, and tasteless. Using a radon detection kit is the only way to detect this radioactive gas. You can purchase an inexpensive kit to measure the radon level in the basement of your home or other building. If you detect an elevated level, check the Internet as to what steps can be taken to reduce the amount of radon.

Why Is Salt Spread on Icy Roads?

BACKGROUND INFORMATION

Sand and salt are often spread on icy roads. Sand provides better traction so that cars are less likely to skid. Salt is used for a different reason. Salt causes the ice to melt. Salt melts ice by lowering the freezing point of water. The freezing point of a substance is defined as the temperature at which a substance exists in both the liquid and solid states. Note that the freezing point of a substance is the same as its melting point.

Assume that the temperature is 32°F, which is the freezing point of water. Ice will form on roads at this temperature. If salt lowers the freezing point, then ice should not form at this temperature.

Hypothesis
Salt lowers the freezing point of water.

Materials
- Adult helper
- Nail
- Styrofoam™ cup
- Ice cubes
- Towel
- Cutting board
- Hammer
- Skewer
- Large empty can with top removed
- Gooseneck lamp (optional)
- Measuring cup
- Teaspoon
- Salt

Procedure
1. Use the nail to poke four small holes in the bottom of the cup.
2. Use the nail to poke two holes near the top of the cup exactly opposite one another.
3. Wrap some ice cubes in a towel. Place the towel on a cutting board. Ask an adult to use the hammer to crush the ice.
4. Fill the cup with the crushed ice to a level just beneath the two holes at the top.
5. Insert the skewer through the two holes.
6. Place the skewer so that the cup hangs freely inside the large can.
7. Place the paper cup in direct sunlight or under the lamp.
8. Allow the ice to melt for 30 minutes.
9. Remove the cup from the can.
10. Pour the water inside the can into a measuring cup. Record the volume of water.
11. Repeat steps 4–9, but this time, add 2 teaspoons of salt to the crushed ice. Be sure to place the same amount of ice in the cup.

Results
More water collects in the can when salt is added.

Conclusion and Explanation
Salt lowers the freezing point of water. Therefore, at a given temperature, a mixture of salt and ice will melt faster than just ice alone.

SECONDARY EXPERIMENT

The freezing point of water is called a colligative property. A colligative property does not depend on what substance is added. Rather a colligative property depends on how much of the substance is added. For example, adding 4 teaspoons of salt should lower the freezing point more than adding 2 teaspoons. In addition, you might think that adding 4 teaspoons of another substance such as baking soda would have the same effect on the freezing point of water as adding 4 teaspoons of salt.

However, the substance that is added must dissolve in water to affect its freezing point. For this reason, adding baking soda, gravel, or sand—items that do not dissolve in water—does not have any effect on the freezing point of water.

Modify the main experiment to show that the freezing point of water is a colligative property.

Why Is Air Considered a Fluid?

BACKGROUND INFORMATION

Three states of matter exist—solid, liquid, and gas. A solid has a definite shape and a definite volume. A liquid has a definite volume but not a definite shape. A gas has neither a definite shape nor a definite volume. Mention the word fluid, and most people think of liquids such as water or fruit juice. All liquids are fluids. However, not all fluids are liquids. A fluid is a substance that can flow. Because solids do not flow, they are not considered fluids. However, both liquids and gases do flow. Therefore, fluids include not only liquids but also gases.

Air is a mixture of gases. Therefore, air is a fluid. The following experiment shows how to demonstrate that air is a fluid by proving that it flows.

Hypothesis

If air is a fluid, then it must flow.

Materials

- Candle (votive candle works best)
- Plate
- Tablespoon
- Baking soda
- Large measuring cup
- White vinegar
- Poster board (4 inches by 12 inches)

Procedure

1. Light the candle and place it on the plate.
2. Add 1 tablespoon of baking soda to the measuring cup.
3. Add ¼ cup of white vinegar to the baking soda.
4. Describe what happens.
5. Fold the poster board in half lengthwise to make a long trough.
6. Wait until the fizzing action inside the cup begins to slow down.
7. Hold the trough at an angle with one end near the candle.
8. Use your other hand to pour the air inside the measuring cup down the trough. Be sure not to pour any liquid down the trough.
9. Describe what happens to the flame.

Results

Gas bubbles form when the vinegar is added to the baking soda. Pouring the air down the trough extinguishes the flame.

Conclusion and Explanation

Air is a fluid because it flows. Mixing vinegar and baking soda produces carbon dioxide gas, which are the tiny bubbles that form. Carbon dioxide is one of the gases in air. Carbon dioxide is heavier than air so it flows down the trough. A flame needs oxygen to burn. The carbon dioxide replaces all the oxygen so the flame can no longer burn. Carbon dioxide is used in fire extinguishers because it is effective in smothering flames.

SECONDARY EXPERIMENT

The mixture of gases in air includes carbon dioxide, nitrogen, and oxygen. These gases are present in different amounts. Nitrogen makes up most of the air. The following experiment shows how you can calculate the percentage of air made up of oxygen.

Materials
- Adult helper
- Narrow empty spice jar (slightly taller than a birthday candle with a mouth that can be covered by a quarter)
- Measuring cup
- Matches
- Birthday candle
- Quarter
- Saucer
- Marker

Procedure
1. Fill the jar with water.
2. Determine the volume of the water in the jar by pouring the water into the measuring cup.
3. Ask the adult to light the candle and drip a few drops of melted wax on the quarter.
4. Stand the candle on the quarter until the melted wax holds it firmly in place.
5. Pour the water into the saucer.
6. Place the quarter with the candle upright in the saucer.
7. Ask the adult to light the candle.
8. Ask the adult to place the jar upside down over the burning candle.
9. Describe what happens.
10. When the candle goes out, mark the level of the water in the jar.
11. Remove the jar.
12. Pour water into the jar up to the mark.

13. Determine the volume of water in the jar by pouring the water into the measuring cup.

Results
As the candle burns, water moves into the jar.

Conclusion and Explanation
As the candle burns, oxygen in the air inside the jar is used up. Water moves into the jar to fill the space once occupied by the oxygen.

The volume of water in the jar equals the volume of air in the jar. The volume of water that moves into the jar equals the volume of oxygen in the jar that is used up as the candle burns. You can calculate the percentage of oxygen in air by using the following equation.

$$\text{Percent of oxygen in air} = \frac{\text{volume of oxygen in jar}}{\text{volume of air in jar}} \times 100$$

Oxygen makes up about 21 percent of air. How does your calculation compare to this value? Your value may not agree for several reasons. For example, not all the oxygen may be used up even though the candle no longer burns. A conclusion is more valid if the experiment is repeated several times. Repeat this experiment several times to see how your results compare.

How Can You Get Light to Flow?

BACKGROUND INFORMATION

Both liquids and gases are fluids because they flow. The following experiment shows how you can get light to flow. Is light then considered a fluid? The answer is no. In the following experiment, the light does not really flow. Light appears to flow because of a property known as reflection.

Reflection involves changing the direction in which light rays travel. A mirror reflects light rays very well. The following experiment will show you that water can also reflect light rays. In fact, water can reflect light rays so well that it appears to light up.

Hypothesis

Light rays can be reflected so that water appears to light up.

Materials

- Hammer
- Nail
- Empty baby food jar with screw-on lid
- Electrical tape
- Flashlight
- Small bowl

Procedure

1. Use the hammer and nail to punch two holes through the lid. The holes should be opposite each other.
2. Tape the bulb end of the flashlight to the bottom of the jar. Make sure that the tape completely covers the jar.
3. Fill the jar with water and screw on the lid.
4. Place the bowl on a counter top or table.
5. Darken the room.
6. Turn on the flashlight and tilt it so that water slowly pours into the bowl.
7. Look at the water as it flows into the bowl. Describe what you see.

Results

The water lights up as it flows. The water that collects in the bowl may also appear to light up.

Conclusion and Explanation

The water appears to light up because of the reflection of light rays. The tape around the jar prevents the light from passing out through the glass. Instead, the light rays pass through the water in the jar. The light rays continue to pass through the water as it flows from the jar. The stream of water acts like a tunnel by bouncing the light rays back and forth. As a result, the light rays are continuously reflected and seem to pour just like the water.

SECONDARY EXPERIMENT

In the main experiment, the lights rays were reflected by the water so that they stayed inside the stream of water. This is known as total internal reflection. Fiber optic cables use total internal reflection to carry light signals at very high speeds. You can mimic how a fiber optic cable operates by carrying out the following experiment. You must ask an adult to help you with this experiment as you will need to use a laser light. Staring at a laser light can cause eye damage. Although the laser light is safe to use as part of this experiment, it must never be pointed at someone.

Materials

- Adult helper
- Clear flexible plastic tubing (½-inch diameter, 1 yard in length)
- Cup with spout
- Milk
- Red laser diode pointer
- Plastic wrap
- Masking tape

Procedure

1. Ask an adult to hold both ends of the tubing to form a U-shape.
2. Slowly pour water into the tubing so that it is almost full.
3. Add a little milk so that the water is slightly cloudy.
4. Shine the laser light into one end of the tubing.
5. Notice how the light travels through the tubing.
6. Seal one end of the tubing with plastic wrap and tape.
7. Ask the adult to bend the tubing into different shapes.
8. Shine the laser light into the tubing and describe what happens each time.

Results

The laser light bends to follow the shape of the tubing.

Conclusion and Explanation

The laser light follows the bends in the plastic tubing because of total internal reflection. However, you can make a bend so tight that the laser light will not experience total internal reflection. This experiment is a model of how light signals can be transmitted through a fiber optic cable over thousands of miles in less than a second.

What Did Galileo Really Drop?

BACKGROUND INFORMATION

Many people have heard the story about an Italian scientist named Galilei Galileo dropping objects from the top of the Leaning Tower of Pisa. At the time, some 400 years ago, people believed that the heavier or bigger an object was, the faster it would fall. Some stories say that Galileo dropped a musket ball and a cannon ball. The facts are not as clear in other stories. In fact, scientists are not even sure that Galileo dropped anything from the Leaning Tower of Pisa.

In any case, Galileo did perform experiments that led to the discovery that all objects fall toward Earth at the same rate. In other words, heavier objects do not fall faster than lighter objects. Objects fall because of gravity.

Hypothesis

Gravity causes all objects to fall at the same rate.

Materials

- String
- High place from which to safely drop balls, such as a second-story window
- Scissors
- Measuring tape
- Golf ball
- Softball
- Stopwatch
- Calculator
- Basketball

Procedure

1. Hang the string from your dropping point so that it touches the ground.
2. Cut the string and measure its length.
3. Have your helper hold the golf ball and softball at the same height from the dropping point.
4. Say "Drop" and start the stopwatch at the same time.
5. Time how long it takes for the balls to strike the ground.
6. Repeat steps 3–5 four more times.
7. Based on your five results, calculate the average time it takes for the balls to drop.
8. Repeat steps 3–7, using a golf ball and basketball.
9. Repeat steps 3–7, using a softball and basketball.

Results

All the balls hit the ground at about the same time.

Conclusion and Explanation

Gravity causes all objects to fall at the same rate. You may find that both balls do not hit the ground exactly at the same time. Several factors can account for this result. The person may not release both balls at exactly the same time. In addition, there is another force at work in this

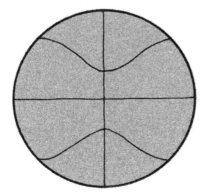

experiment. Each object must push aside air as it falls to the ground. A larger object must push aside more air. The resistance that a falling object meets is called air resistance. A larger object encounters more air resistance, which slows its fall more than a smaller object. However, in the absence of air resistance, all objects fall at exactly the same rate. Scientists have proven this by dropping objects in a vacuum. A vacuum is an enclosed space where all the air has been pumped out.

A moving object, such as any object you dropped, has both speed and velocity. Both are measured as the distance traveled in a given time. However, velocity must also include direction. For example, the speed may be 55 miles per hour, but the velocity is 55 miles per hour heading west. Acceleration is a change in velocity in a given time period.

You can calculate the acceleration of the objects you dropped. The following is the formula for acceleration.

$$\text{acceleration} = \frac{\text{final velocity} - \text{initial velocity}}{\text{time}}$$

Velocity is calculated as follows.

$$\text{velocity} = \frac{\text{distance traveled}}{\text{time}}$$

Assume that a ball takes 2 seconds to fall 120 feet. Its final velocity is 120 feet/2 seconds or 60 feet/second downward. Its initial velocity is zero because the ball was not moving. Therefore, the acceleration of the ball is calculated as follows.

$$\text{acceleration} = \frac{60 \text{ feet/second} - 0 \text{ feet/second}}{2 \text{ seconds}} = 30 \text{ feet/s}^2$$

The above formula involves multiplying second times second (60 feet/second times ½, the reciprocal of 2 seconds). As a result, the unit for acceleration is feet/second squared or feet/s^2. Acceleration due to gravity is 32 feet/s^2. How do your results compare to this value?

What Else Did Newton Discover?

BACKGROUND INFORMATION

Newton is considered by many people to be one of the greatest scientists in history. One reason for this praise are the many major discoveries that Newton made by carefully conducting experiments. Many of these experiments involved the study of matter and how it behaves. His experiments led to three laws that describe how matter behaves. Newton's first law can be stated in the following way: "An object at rest tends to remain at rest, and an object in motion tends to remain in motion with the same speed and in the same direction unless an unbalanced force is applied to the objects." This rather lengthy statement is also known as Newton's Law of Inertia. The following experiment shows how you can perform some magic tricks because of Newton's first law or the Law of Inertia.

Hypothesis

An object at rest tends to remain at rest unless an unbalanced force is applied to the object.

Materials

- Playing card
- Quarter
- Large empty plastic soda or water bottle with cap
- Cloth with no hems or seams

Procedure

1. Hold your hand so that your palm faces upward.
2. Form a fist, and then extend your forefinger.
3. Balance the playing card on the tip of your forefinger.
4. Place the quarter in the center of the card so that they both balance on your finger.
5. Use your other hand to flick the card so that it flies off your finger. Be sure to flick the card so that it flies straight off your finger and not in an upward or downward direction.
6. What happens to the quarter?
7. Fill the bottle with water and put the cap on tightly.
8. Make sure that the outside of the bottle is dry and that it does not leak.
9. Place the cloth on the table so that part of it hangs over the edge.
10. Place the bottle on the table in the center of the cloth.
11. Hold your arms level with the top of the table and grab the part of the cloth hanging over the edge of the table.
12. As quickly as you can, yank the cloth from beneath the bottle. Be sure not to pull upward or downward on the cloth when you yank it.
13. What happens to the bottle?

Results

When you flick the card, the quarter remains balanced on your finger. When you yank the cloth, the bottle filled with water remains on the table. However, at some point when the bottle has less water, the bottle will fall from the table.

Conclusion and Explanation

The card, quarter, cloth, and bottle all have inertia. As a result, they will remain at rest unless an unbalanced force is applied. The card flies from your finger because of the force applied by your other finger. The cloth flies from the table because of the force applied as you yank it. However, no force is applied to the quarter or bottle. As a result, they remain in place.

You may have to practice to get the tricks to work. The secret is to make sure that a force is not applied to either the quarter or the bottle. For example, if you flick the card upward or downward, a force will be applied to the quarter. If you yank the towel in an upward or downward motion, no matter how slight, a force will be applied to the bottle.

SECONDARY EXPERIMENT

Newton also discovered the relationship between the force, mass, and acceleration of an object. His findings led to his second law, which is written as a mathematical formula: $F = ma$.

This equation is read as "The force exerted by an object is equal to its mass times its acceleration." Newton's second law explains why the lemon made a bigger splash than the pea in the "*Gravity* and *Acceleration*" experiment.

Newton's third law is often stated as "For every action, there is an equal and opposite reaction." This law explains how a rocket is launched into space, why a bird can fly through the air, and how a boat moves through the water. You can see Newton's third law in operation by carrying out the following experiment.

Materials
- Two chairs
- 25 feet of fishing line
- Plastic straw
- Balloon
- Tape

Procedure
1. Place each chair at opposite ends of the room.
2. Tie the fishing line to one chair. Thread a plastic straw through the line, and then tie the free end of the line to the other chair. Be sure that the string is stretched tight between the two chairs.
3. Slide the star so that it is close to one of the chairs.
4. Blow up the balloon so that it is about half full of air. Pinch the opening so that the air cannot escape.
5. Tape the plastic straw to the balloon so that the opening points toward the chair close to the straw.
6. Release the opening and watch what happens to the balloon.
7. Repeat steps 4–6 but this time blow up the balloon so that it is full of air.
8. Again observe what happens to the balloon.

Results
The balloon flies along the string, traveling faster and farther when it is filled with air.

Conclusion and Explanation
Air rushes out the opening of the balloon. This air rushes in one direction, causing the balloon to move in the opposite direction. A rocket is a chamber filled with gases. When the gases are ignited, they rush out tiny openings at one end of the rocket, creating a tremendous thrust that pushes the rocket in the opposite direction. Both the balloon and rocket move because of Newton's third law.

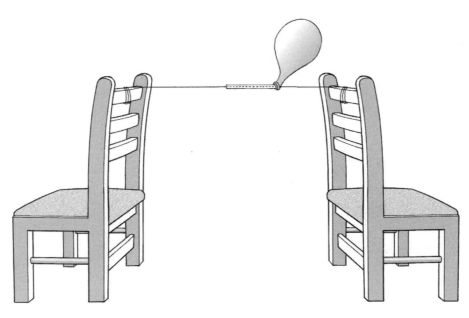

What Do All Moving Objects Have?

BACKGROUND INFORMATION

In addition to speed, velocity, and acceleration, all moving objects have momentum. You have probably heard the word momentum applied to a sports team. A team that is on a winning streak is said to have momentum.

Scientists define momentum as the mass of an object times its velocity (momentum = mass x velocity). Therefore, an object, no matter how large it is, has zero momentum if it is not moving. If all the players on a team were not moving, they would have zero momentum, no matter how many games they have won.

The following experiment explores the relationship between mass, velocity, and momentum. You will determine the momentum of a rolling marble by measuring how far it can move a plastic cup.

Hypothesis

If you increase either the mass or velocity, the momentum will also increase.

Materials

- Scissors
- Plastic cup
- Four marbles
- Two books
- Ruler with groove
- Measuring tape

Procedure

1. Cut a section from the lip of the cup large enough for a marble to pass through.
2. Place the book on the floor and set one end of the ruler on the book to make a ramp that is at least 2 inches high.
3. Place the cup upside down on the floor so that the opening is against the other end of the ruler.
4. Position a marble in the groove of the ruler at the top of the ramp.
5. Release the marble.
6. Measure the distance the cup moved.
7. Repeat steps 4–6 four more times and average your results.
8. Repeat steps 4–6 five times using two marbles and average your results.
9. Repeat steps 4–6 fives times with three marbles and average your results.
10. Repeat steps 4–6 fives times with four marbles and average your results.
11. Place the second book on top of the first one to increase the height of the ramp.
12. Repeat steps 4–10.

Results

The cup moves farther when more marbles hit it. The cup also moves farther when one or more marbles are released from a greater height.

Conclusion and Explanation

An increase in mass (more marbles) or an increase in velocity (higher ramp) increases the momentum of a moving object. The momentum of the rolling marbles was transferred to the cup, which then moved as a result of this transfer of momentum. The more momentum that is transferred, the greater the distance the cup moves.

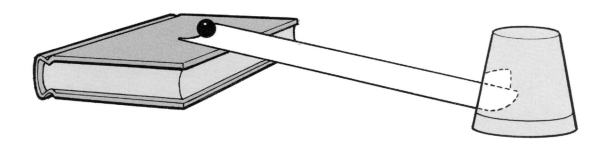

SECONDARY EXPERIMENT

You have probably seen figure skaters pull in their arms as they spin. When they do this, they spin faster. An object that is spinning around a fixed point has a momentum known as angular momentum. Angular momentum depends on how far out the object extends and its velocity. Angular momentum is conserved when skaters pull in their arms. When the distance an object extends is decreased, its velocity must increase.

Materials

• Two metal washers
• 3-foot length of string
• Plastic shell from a ballpoint pen (remove all the inside pieces)

Procedure
1. Tie the washers to one end of the string.

2. Pass the free end of the string through shell of the pen.
3. Use one hand to hold the free end of the string.
4. Use your other hand to hold the plastic shell and start swinging the washers.
5. Use your hand to lower and raise the string.
6. Observe changes in the velocity of the washers as your bring them closer to the shell.

Results
The velocity of the swinging washers increases as they move closer to the plastic shell.

Conclusion and Explanation
The angular momentum of an object is conserved as it moves. As the distance the object extends decreases, its velocity must increase in order to maintain its angular momentum. This is why figure skaters pull in their arms to spin faster.

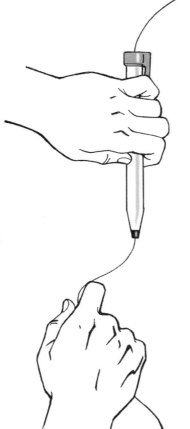

What Helps You to Digest Food?

BACKGROUND INFORMATION

Digestion involves both physical and chemical changes. Physical changes occur in the mouth when the teeth break apart food into smaller pieces. Chemical changes occur in the stomach when cells secrete enzymes that break down the food into new substances. An enzyme is a chemical found in a living thing, which speeds up a chemical reaction. An enzyme can make a chemical reaction occur thousands of times faster than it would without the enzyme. You can check how enzymes speed up the digestion of proteins by carrying out the following experiment.

Hypothesis

If an enzyme is present, digestion will occur at a faster rate.

Materials

- Gelatin dessert
- Knife
- Ruler
- Five small clear drinking glasses
- Masking tape
- Marker
- Teaspoon
- Meat tenderizer
- Measuring cup
- Apple juice
- Pineapple juice
- Orange juice

Procedure

1. Prepare the gelatin dessert according to the instructions. Refrigerate until it solidifies.
2. Cut five 1-inch square pieces of solid gelatin. Save the remaining gelatin if you plan on doing the Secondary Experiment.
3. Place each piece of gelatin in a separate glass. Use the tape and marker to label the glasses 1, 2, 3, 4, and 5.
4. Dissolve 1 teaspoon of meat tenderizer in 4 ounces of water.
5. Add the following to the glasses: 4 ounces of water into #1; 4 ounces of apple juice into #2; 4 ounces of pineapple juice into #3; 4 ounces of orange juice into #4; 4 ounces of the meat tenderizer solution into #5.
6. Allow the gelatin pieces to soak in the solutions for 24 hours.
7. Describe the appearance of each gelatin piece.

Results

The gelatin cubes remain unchanged in the water, apple juice, and orange juice glasses. The gelatin cubes are smaller, or even absent, in the pineapple juice and meat tenderizer glasses.

Conclusion and Explanation

The gelatin is digested in the glasses containing pineapple juice and meat tenderizer. As the gelatin is digested, the cube gets smaller. No digestion takes place in the glasses containing water, apple juice, and orange juice.

Like meat, gelatin is made from proteins. Meat tenderizer is sprinkled on meat to soften it. The tenderizer contains an enzyme that breaks down the proteins in meat to new substances called amino acids. Pineapples also contain an enzyme that speeds up the chemical digestion of the proteins in the gelatin. This enzyme is not present in water, apple juice, or orange juice.

#1 Water

#2 Apple Juice

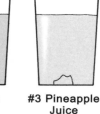
#3 Pineapple Juice

#4 Orange Juice

#5 Meat Tenderizer

SECONDARY EXPERIMENT

Enzymes work best if certain conditions are met. One of these conditions is the proper temperature. Find out which temperature is best for the enzyme that digests the proteins in gelatin.

Materials
- Gelatin dessert (use any remaining from the main experiment)
- Knife
- Ruler
- Three small clear drinking glasses
- Pineapple juice
- Measuring cup
- Refrigerator
- Gooseneck lamp
- Thermometer

Procedure
1. Add a 1-inch cube of gelatin to each glass.
2. Pour 4 ounces of pineapple juice into each glass.
3. Place one glass in the refrigerator. Place another glass directly under the lamp. Keep the third glass at room temperature.
4. Check the glasses after 24 hours and record your observations.
5. Measure the temperature of the pineapple juice in each glass.

Results
The gelatin cube placed under the lamp is the smallest. The gelatin cube left at room temperature is smaller than it was. The gelatin cube in the refrigerator shows little, if any, change in size. The temperature of the pineapple juice is coldest in the refrigerator, warmer at room temperature, and even warmer under the lamp.

Conclusion and Explanation
The enzyme in pineapple juice that digests proteins works best in warmer temperatures. The stomach enzymes that digest proteins work best at around 98.6° F. Lowering and raising the temperature from this point reduces the enzyme's ability to digest proteins.

The function of an enzyme depends on its shape. Changing the temperature changes the shape of an enzyme. The more the temperature is changed, the more the shape of the enzyme is changed. Because its shape has been changed, the enzyme cannot work as well.

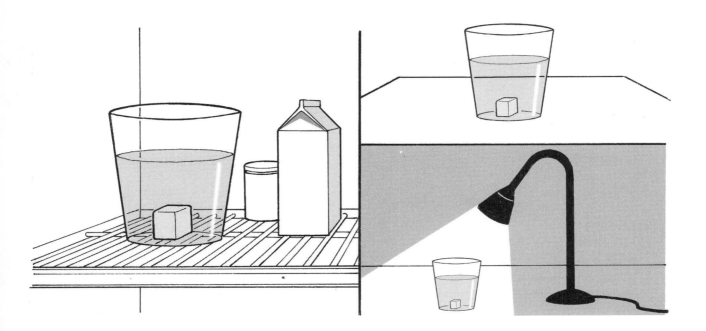

What Do You Need to Stay Healthy?

BACKGROUND INFORMATION

To stay healthy, a person must eat foods that will provide everything the body needs, including certain vitamins. Vitamins are essential for good health. They are needed only in small amounts to perform certain key roles in the body. For example, vitamin C is needed by the body to make a substance called collagen. Collagen can be considered the "cement" that connects and binds cells so that they can work together as a unit.

Most people get the vitamin C they need from fruits and vegetables. Another source of vitamin C is orange juice. You can easily test orange juice and other beverages to see if they contain vitamin C. This test uses corn starch and iodine. Iodine reacts with starch to produce a blue-black color. However, iodine reacts with vitamin C before it reacts with iodine. You can use this difference to find out which juice contains the most vitamin C.

Hypothesis

Not all juices and beverages contain the same amount of vitamin C.

Materials

- Tablespoon
- Cornstarch
- Measuring cup
- Pot
- Stove
- Coffee filter
- Bowl
- Orange juice
- Small clear drinking glass
- Teaspoon
- Tincture of iodine
- Dropper or straw

Procedure

1. Add 1 tablespoon of cornstarch to 2 cups of water in a pot.
2. Gently boil the water for 2 minutes.
3. Allow the cornstarch solution to cool.
4. Pour the solution through a coffee filter into the bowl.
5. Pour 4 ounces of water into the glass.
6. Add 1 teaspoon of the cornstarch solution to the water and stir.
7. Add the iodine a drop at a time to the water-cornstarch solution. You can use a narrow straw if you do not have a dropper. Place an index finger over an open end and dip the straw into the iodine. Hold the straw over the glass and slowly lift your finger until a drop is released. You may want to practice by using the straw to release water one drop at a time.

8. Swirl the glass after adding each drop of iodine. Continue adding the iodine until the solution turns a blue-black color. If you add too much iodine, the solution will turn brown.
9. Rinse the glass.
10. Pour 4 ounces of the orange juice into the glass.
11. Add 1 teaspoon of the starch solution to the juice and stir.
12. Record how many drops of iodine you add to turn the juice-cornstarch solution a blue-black color.
13. Rinse the glass.
14. Repeat steps 9–12, but this time, test another brand of juice or a different beverage, such as apple juice.

Results

Iodine reacts with cornstarch to produce a blue-black color. However, more drops of iodine are needed to produce a blue-black color when cornstarch is mixed with an orange juice that contains vitamin C. The number of drops of iodine needed depends on the beverage tested.

Conclusion and Explanation

Not all beverages contain the same amount of vitamin C. Assume that one juice contains twice as much vitamin C as another juice. If cornstarch is added to both these juices, then the one that has twice as much vitamin C will require twice as many drops of iodine to turn blue-black compared to the other juice.

SECONDARY EXPERIMENT

Vitamins and minerals are sometimes added to foods. Such foods are sometimes called "enriched" or "fortified." Iron is one substance that is often added to enrich or fortify foods such as breads and cereals. The body needs iron to make hemoglobin, which is found in red blood cells where it transports oxygen. If the body does not get enough iron, a condition known as anemia may result.

Only a small amount of iron is needed to enable hemoglobin to transport sufficient oxygen. Well-balanced meals usually provide this amount of iron. However, some people may require additional iron, which can be obtained by taking iron supplement pills or eating food that contain added iron. The following experiment involves taking out the iron that is added to certain cereals.

Materials

- Small magnet painted white
- Measuring cup
- Iron-fortified cereal (check the label)
- Tablespoon
- Magnifying lens

Procedure

1. Place the magnet in the bowl.
2. Add 1 cup of cereal in the bowl.
3. Use the spoon to crush the cereal.
4. Add 2 cups of hot water.
5. Allow the cereal to soak for 30 minutes.
6. Stir the cereal and water for 5-10 minutes.
7. Use the spoon to remove the magnet from the bowl.
8. Examine the magnet with the magnifying lens.
9. Describe the appearance of the magnet.

Results

The magnet is dotted with black specks.

Conclusion and Explanation

The magnet attracted the iron that was present in the cereal. You can test different cereals to see which one contains the most iron.

How High Will Your Geyser Soar?

BACKGROUND INFORMATION

A geyser occurs when hot water from an underground source erupts into the air. Three conditions must be met for a geyser to erupt. First, there must be an abundant supply of water. Second, there must be a source of intense heat. This heat usually comes from magma, or molten rock. Third, the underground rock formation must act like a pressure cooker, storing the water until it reaches a temperature above its boiling point.

These three conditions exist in only a few places on Earth. One such place is Yellowstone National Park, which has the world's most famous geyser, Old Faithful. Yellowstone is home to more than half the world's geysers, which number only about one thousand in all. However, you can build your own geyser anytime you want by carrying out the following experiment. Make sure to test your geyser outdoors so that it soars high into the air just like a real one.

Hypothesis

A model of a geyser can be built using household products.

Materials

- 2-liter bottle of carbonated soda
- Plastic wrap
- Small nail
- Strong sewing needle
- Sugar candies (Mentos® candies work well) or mints
- Thread
- Tape
- Scissors

Procedure

1. Remove the cap from the bottle. Cover the mouth of the bottle with plastic wrap.
2. Use the nail to poke a narrow hole, no larger than ¼ inch, in the bottle cap.
3. Use the needle to poke a hole through six candies.
4. Thread the needle. Then pass the needle through the hole in each candy so that the candies are arranged like beads on a string.
5. Cut the string, leaving enough to tie a knot at the end. Make sure that the knot is large enough so that it cannot pass through the holes in the candies.
6. Pass the needle through the hole in the bottle cap from the bottom.
7. The candies must hang as closely as possible to the bottom of the cap. Tape the thread to the top of the bottle cap to hold the candies in place.
8. Remove the plastic wrap from the bottle. Carefully feed the candies through the mouth of the bottle and screw the cap back on the bottle. Make sure that the candies hang freely from the cap but do not come in contact with the soda.
9. Remove the tape from the bottle cap so that the candies fall into the soda.
10. Stand back and watch.

Results

Like a geyser, the soda erupts into the air.

Conclusion and Explanation

The candies cause the soda to erupt like a geyser. The soda contains carbon dioxide gas. As long as the bottle is capped, the gas remains as tiny bubbles trapped in the liquid. If the cap is removed, the bubbles will slowly rise to the surface where the gas escapes. An uncapped bottle of soda goes "flat" because all the gas bubbles eventually escape.

To escape, the gas bubbles must rise to the surface. However, the water in the soda traps the gas bubbles, keeping them in the liquid. As a result, the bubbles rise very slowly to the surface. However, the candies make it easy for the gas bubbles to get past the water and rise quickly to the surface. When they do, the gas bubbles create a pressure that forces them out the tiny opening in the cap. The gas bubbles then soar into the air, just like a geyser.

SECONDARY EXPERIMENT

The water that erupts in a geyser eventually seeps back down into the ground. The water will seep through the ground at different rates, depending on the nature of the soil. Tiny spaces, or pores, are present in the soil to allow the water to seep downward through the ground. The space these pores take up is known as the pore volume. The pore volume varies, depending on the type of soil. In the following experiment, you will calculate the pore volume of a sample of sand.

Materials
- Marking pen
- Two empty 2-liter plastic soda bottles (one must have a cap)
- Scissors
- Ruler
- Measuring cup
- Piece of wire screening
- Sand

Procedure
1. Label one bottle #1 and the other bottle #2.
2. Screw the cap on bottle #1 and remove the label.
3. Cut off the bottom 2 inches from the base.
4. Turn the bottle upside down.
5. Pour 4 ounces of water into the bottle.
6. Mark the level of the water on the outside of the bottle.
7. Continue adding 4 ounces of water at a time and mark each level (8 ounces, 12 ounces, etc.) on the bottle.
8. Pour out the water.
9. Cut a 2-inch square of screening and wad it into a ball.
10. Insert the screen ball into the neck of the bottle.
11. Fill the bottle with dry sand to the 32-ounce mark.
12. Pour 1 quart (32 ounces) of water into bottle #2.

13. Slowly pour the water into bottle #1 so that it seeps through the sand.
14. Continue pouring until the water can be seen just rising at the surface of the sand.
15. Measure the volume of water still left in bottle #2.
16. Calculate the pore volume of the sand by using the following formula:

$$\text{pore volume} = 32 \text{ ounces [original volume of water]} - x \text{ ounces [volume left in bottle \#2]}$$

Results
As an example, if the volume of water still left in bottle #2 is 10 ounces, then the pore volume is calculated as follows:

$$\text{pore volume} = 32 \text{ ounces} - 10 \text{ ounces} = 22 \text{ ounces}$$

In other words, the pores present in 32 ounces of sand hold 22 ounces of water.

Conclusion and Explanation
The pore volume varies, depending on the type of soil. The shape and arrangement of the particles in the soil determine its pore volume. Generally, soils have a pore volume that ranges between 20 and 50 percent of their volume. In other words, 32 ounces of a soil sample would hold between 6.4 and 16 ounces of water. You can check the pore volumes of different soils. Repeat steps 10–16 using different types of soil such as topsoil, clay, and samples taken from different areas in your community.

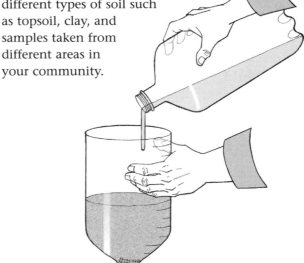

How Did the Egyptians Make Mummies?

BACKGROUND INFORMATION

All sorts of products come with a small packet that contains silica gel. The purpose of the silica gel is to absorb moisture. The silica gel is known as a desiccant. Silica gel can absorb about 40 percent of its weight in moisture. Absorbing all this moisture prevents vitamin pills stored in a plastic bottle from spoiling and electronic parts in a new camera from rusting.

The Egyptians used a desiccant for an entirely different purpose. They used it to prepare their mummies. The desiccant they used is called natron, a natural substance the Egyptians obtained from the shores and bottoms of lakes. Natron absorbed moisture that would otherwise promote the growth of bacteria, including those that are known as decomposers. The following experiment will show how a desiccant absorbs moisture and prevents bacteria from growing.

Hypothesis

A desiccant prevents the growth of bacteria.

Materials

- Knife
- Apple
- Two large plastic cups
- Measuring cup
- Baking soda
- Salt
- Mixing bowl

Procedure

1. Cut the apple into quarters.
2. Place two apple slices in each cup.

3. Mix ¼ cup of baking soda and ¼ cup of salt in the bowl.
4. Pour the baking soda and salt over the apple slices in one cup.
5. Place the cups in an area not in direct sunlight and wait 5–7 days.
6. Pour off the baking soda and salt.
7. Compare the appearance of the apple slices in both cups.

Results

The apple left exposed to the air decomposed. The skin on the apple covered by the baking soda and salt may appear black and shrunken. However, the apple itself did not rot or spoil.

Conclusion and Explanation

Baking soda and salt can prevent spoilage and decomposition. They act as a desiccant by absorbing the moisture that would otherwise promote the growth of decomposing bacteria.

SECONDARY EXPERIMENT

You can expand the main experiment to find the best desiccant. In addition to baking soda and salt, you can use baking powder, Epsom salts, and kosher salt. Try varying the proportions of each ingredient. You can also test your desiccants on various fruits to see if they preserve some better than others. If you have a kitchen scale, you can weigh the fruit before and after to see how much water was absorbed by the desiccant. Any loss in weight represents the water that has been absorbed by the desiccant.

Why Does Food Spoil?

Hypothesis

Salt and vinegar can preserve foods.

Materials

- Teaspoon
- Chicken bouillon cube
- Measuring cup
- Three clear jars
- Labeling tape
- Marker
- Plastic wrap

Procedure

1. Use the spoon to dissolve the bouillon cube in one cup of hot water.
2. Pour ⅓ cup of the bouillon into each of the three jars.
3. Add 1 teaspoon of salt to one jar and stir. Seal the jar with plastic wrap. Rinse the spoon. Label the jar "salt."
4. Add 1 teaspoon of vinegar to another jar and stir. Seal the jar with plastic wrap. Label the jar "vinegar."
5. Seal the third jar with plastic wrap. Label the jar "control."
6. Place the jars in a warm place for three days. Each day, describe the appearance of the bouillon in each jar.
7. Pour the bouillon down a sink and thoroughly wash the jars with soap and water.

Results

The jar labeled "control" appears the cloudiest. The jar labeled "salt" appears cloudy. The jar labeled "vinegar" appears almost as clear as it was at the start of the experiment.

Conclusion and Explanation

After three days, the bouillon changes the most in appearance when nothing is added to it. The bouillon changes slightly in appearance when salt is added. The bouillon changes little, if at all, when vinegar is added.

The cloudiness is caused by bacteria that grow in the bouillon. These microorganisms feed on nutrients in the bouillon. Salt helps to preserve the bouillon by reducing the number of bacteria that grow. Vinegar is a better preserver because even fewer bacteria grow in the bouillon. Repeat this experiment, but this time place the jars in a refrigerator. How does refrigeration affect the growth of bacteria?

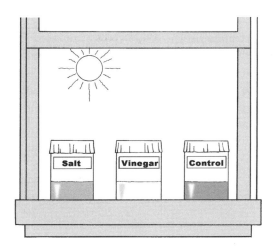

SECONDARY EXPERIMENT

Today, other chemicals have replaced salt and vinegar as preservatives. For example, if you check the label on a loaf of bread, you may see the words "calcium propionate." Check the list of ingredients on a box of pie or cake mix, and you will probably see the words "sodium propionate." Both these chemicals are preservatives.

These chemicals are added to prevent mold from growing on the bread, pie, or cake. Mold is the greenish substance that appears on these products when they spoil. Adding the preservatives allows these products to have a longer shelf life. However, many people prefer to eat bread that does not contain any preservatives. The following experiment will explore how well preservatives in bread work to prevent mold from growing.

Materials
- Two paper napkins
- Two sealable plastic bags
- Bread slice with propionate preservative
- Bread slice without propionate preservative (both breads should have the same expiration date)
- Marker

Procedure
1. Moisten two paper napkins with water and place one in each plastic bag.
2. Place one slice of bread preserved with propionate on the paper napkin in one bag and seal it. Label the bag "with propionate."
3. Place one slice of bread that does not contain any preservative in the other bag and seal it. Label the bag "control."
4. Place both bags in a warm place.

5. Observe the bags every day for mold growth. The mold will grow as greenish or yellowish fibers.
6. Discard the bags without opening them.

Results
Mold first appears on the bread without preservative. The time it takes for mold to appear depends on a number of factors, including how old the bread is, the temperature, and the amount of moisture in the bag. Mold needs water to grow.

Conclusion and Explanation
Propionate retards but does not prevent the growth of mold because mold eventually grows on the bread with preservative. Repeat this experiment, but this time moisten the paper napkins with vinegar. You should find that mold grows sooner than when the napkins were moistened with water. Vinegar is an acid. Propionate does not work as well in an acidic environment.